EMPLOYEE
ENRAGEMENT

CONTENTS

Introduction 1

- #50 **Mood Swings** 3
- #49 **Care and Compassion** 5
- #48 **Lateness** 7
- #47 **Poor Performance Managed Poorly** 9
- #46 **Training and Development** 11
- #45 **Empowerment** 13
- #44 **Decision Delays** 15
- #43 **Technology Breakdowns** 17
- #42 **Ignoring Problems** 19
- #41 **Office Psychopaths** 21
- #40 **Direction and Guidance** 23
- #39 **Goals** 25
- #38 **Boredom** 27
- #37 **Focusing on the Bad** 29
- #36 **Hypocrisy** 31
- #35 **Wasted Talents** 33
- #34 **Taking Credit for Others' Work** 35
- #33 **Constant Changes** 37
- #32 **Pay and Rewards** 39
- #31 **Rudeness and Unfriendliness** 41
- #30 **Process Violations** 43
- #29 **Meritocracy** 45
- #28 **Bureaucracy** 47
- #27 **Overworked** 49
- #26 **Desperately Seeking Support** 51
- #25 **Incompetent Management** 53
- #24 **Input and Consultation** 55
- #23 **Expectations** 57
- #22 **Office Politics** 59
- #21 **Disrespect** 61
- #20 **Listening** 63
- #19 **Dismissing Ideas** 65
- #18 **Personal Performance** 67

#17 **Micromanagement** 69
#16 **Information Overload** 71
#15 **Blame** 73
#14 **Dishonesty** 75
#13 **Broken Promises** 77
#12 **Favouritism** 79
#11 **Condescending & Dictatorial Managers** 81
#10 **Deadlines and Time** 83
#9 **Gossip and Backstabbing** 85
#8 **Team? What Team?** 87
#7 **Annoying and Inconsiderate Co-workers** 89
#6 **Customers** 91
#5 **Negativity** 93
#4 **Accountability and Responsibility** 95
#3 **Communication Issues** 97
#2 **Unappreciated and Unrecognised** 99
#1 **Lazy and Underperforming Co-workers** 101

Uncensored 103

INTRODUCTION

People underestimate the influence that managers have on their employees. What you say and do changes moods, alters lives, shapes personalities, forges careers, inspires performance, and lights the way. Whether you're a Team Leader or a CEO, you are privileged to serve in such a special capacity.

The fact that this book is in your hands is proof that you care enough about the impact you make – or hey, maybe it's just an easy tax deduction, a dud gift, or something else you'll place on your shelf with the other books you haven't read. Regardless, I thank you for trusting me to guide you through this process.

Employee Enragement: Why People Hate Working for You is based on a study of 2,400 employees who were asked: *'What makes you angry, upset, or frustrated at work?'*

And they didn't just *share* – they *shouted*!

About 40 per cent of the respondents were in Australia, another 40 per cent were from the United States, and the rest were spread across other parts of the world. In this book, I expand on the top factors that employees dislike at work, beginning at 50 and counting down to 1.

I recommend you visit my website – jamesadonis.com – and click on *'With Compliments'* where there are free e-books for you to download on how to attract, engage, motivate, and retain your employees.

Wishing you success at work and in life,

James Adonis

#50
MOOD SWINGS

Mood swings. We all have them. One minute we're cheerful, the next minute we're sad – and sometimes for the most insignificant of reasons. It might be the weather, something someone said, or the fact you're still single (that one gets me every time).

Whatever the reason, our moods are impacted. Our body language changes from open to closed, our words change from happy to snappy, and our tone changes from nice to abrupt. We go from Dr Jekyll to Mr Hyde and then back again.

The question is this: *how do you want your employees to feel after they've had contact with you?* If you don't care, then perhaps this isn't the right profession for you. Try horse whispering.

But if you want your employees to walk away from every encounter they have with you feeling better about themselves, better about their abilities, and better about their jobs – basically, if you want the impact you make to be one where people are better off just by being within your team – then you've got to rise above mood swings. Remember, you're always being watched. Spooky, but true.

Whenever you're in a bad mood, think of something that makes you laugh; write down five things you're grateful for; go for a walk to clear your head; get some exercise; play uplifting music; have a joke book nearby; indulge in stuff that makes you feel better like massages or chocolate; and speak positively.

#49 CARE AND COMPASSION

Caring is so interesting to observe. We take greater care of our cars than we do of our bodies. We care more about giving advice than taking it ourselves. We care more about what we don't have than what we already possess. And that same care factor is evident at work. For example, we care more about achieving performance targets than about the employees who'll deliver them.

The reason this mentality exists is because managers are still managing '1970s Style'. If you're no longer wearing flared pants with bright flower prints, driving a Mustang, and watching *The Brady Bunch*, then don't hang on to the old-school style of management. Managers who weren't even born in the 1970s manage '1970s Style' because that's how they've been taught.

Back in the 70s, jobs were rare and candidates were plenty, so managers had the power. They could get away with being uncaring. But now there are fewer candidates and jobs galore, so it's employees who have the power. *And they know it.* They're aware that if they don't have a manager who cares, they can resign today with the confidence they'll easily find one who does.

View your employees as volunteers, rather than as workers; ask them what they need to be more engaged; check up on them regularly to see how they're going; listen to them more; and genuinely appreciate them. If you don't care for and show compassion towards your employees, there's no reason why they should do so for your customers.

#48 LATENESS

I had a job once where I came to work on time on only 14 occasions in 18 months. The remaining 376 days I arrived anywhere between ten minutes and two hours late. It wasn't so much that I was chronologically challenged; it's just that I hated this job to such a degree that I would rather chew on razorblades than be there.

I was lucky no-one ever really noticed. Upon handing in my resignation, my boss said: 'I had a feeling you weren't happy when you came in late once or twice.' *Once or twice?*

People are smart enough to know the impact of coming in late. And yet so many of us continue to guiltily sneak up to our desks without saying 'hi' to our workmates in the hope they'll think we've been there all day.

There are two facets to this: *you* being the late one, and your *employees* being the latecomers. If you're the latecomer, take a look at the ten most recent times you've been late. Write down the reason why you were late for each occasion and you'll notice a pattern emerging. Then take action.

As for your employees, offer incentives for coming on time, provide flexible work options, and penalise the chronic latecomers. Also, employees who *love* their work are usually *early* rather than late, so utilise your employees' natural talents at work, and provide them with challenges, variety, autonomy, and feedback – all of which are the ingredients for job satisfaction.

#47
POOR PERFORMANCE MANAGED POORLY

When I was young, my parents would smack me. Before you judge them, they were (and still are) the most exceptional parents anyone could ever have and I love them dearly, but they preferred to discipline their children in the way many Greek parents do. I'd get smacked in the shopping mall, smacked in the playground, smacked at parties, and there were even times my dad would stop the car on the side of the street just to lend us a 'hand'.

Now, to be perfectly honest, the smacks were never painful. But boy, were they *embarrassing*. And when my sisters and I would turn red, it was never due to the force of my parents' hands, but due to the shame of being disciplined in public.

At work, so many managers smack their employees.

Not literally, of course, but figuratively. They'll give negative feedback in front of others; they'll use harsher penalties than necessary; they'll pass judgement on someone's performance before first asking the employee what might be causing it; they'll demand what they expect but not provide guidance on how to achieve it.

All of these are examples of poor performance being managed poorly. With children, I guess it might be okay to scold them in public – but to adults it's demeaning.

So the next time you stand up from your desk to address an issue with an employee, ask yourself: *Am I about to deliver a public smack?*

#46 TRAINING AND DEVELOPMENT

In management journals there's so much emphasis on the *right* kind of training. There's stuff on personality types, e-learning, coaching, workshops – and it's all great. However, in this entire study, *not once* did anyone mention *anything* about the *type* of training they receive. Nope, they just commented extensively on *not* receiving training *at all*.

There are two kinds of issues with this non-training culture. The first is that people aren't able to do their jobs properly, and the second is that they're unable to develop. It's the equivalent of trying to grow flowers without water, pets without food, or children without The Wiggles.

Consider the brain to be a muscle. The more you exercise it, the stronger it gets. The more you neglect it, the less it's able to function to its capacity. So it really isn't any wonder to see employees becoming lazy and hopeless simply because they're not being stimulated at work anymore.

I'm not going to get into how to deliver a great training program. Google it. My purpose here is to convince you that training is a vital part of employee engagement. It's an investment in your people. Study after study shows that employees would stay longer with a company if they received regular training and development. And yet the average employee receives less than 20 hours of employer-sponsored training every year.

#45 EMPOWERMENT

Many managers confuse *empowerment* with *delegation*. Delegation is giving your employees tasks to do – empowerment is enabling them to think for themselves. Delegation is when employees follow your decisions – empowerment is when they make their own. Delegation is when employees have to obtain your authority – empowerment is when you give *them* the authority.

Think of empowerment as a race. Either you're in a sprint wearing running shoes, or you're in a three-legged race wearing stilettos. Here's the sprinting with running shoes method:

Get ready. Get your employees ready for the additional responsibility by training them. Teach them the fundamentals of making great decisions. Coach them through a few processes and give them feedback. They're often ready for the next challenge before you think they are.

Get set. Put aside your fear of losing power. Recognise you're not the only one who can make the right decisions. Step back, allow your employees to chart their course, and if they approach you to make a decision for them, don't give in. Be available as a support person, but encourage *them* to make the final decisions.

Go! You'll totally undo all empowerment and create a team of cynics if you don't embrace their decisions despite what comes back. Don't act as a level of 'approval', which is the opposite of empowerment. Be prepared for them to make mistakes. Give your employees the room to do work differently than you would. Praise their achievements, results, and efforts.

#44
DECISION DELAYS

It might be delays in making promotional decisions, delays in approving employees' leave requests, or delays in authorising project plans. Whatever it is, while we're busily getting on with our day, there are employees painfully counting the minutes while they await our decisions.

There's a quote by someone called Anonymous (most likely a Greek philosopher) that I love: *'If it weren't for the last minute, nothing would get done.'* So why do we delay certain tasks, especially the task of *deciding*?

It's not a priority. Then say so. Provide your employees with realistic and fair turnaround times for your decisions, and touch base with them in advance if you feel you won't be able to meet their expectations.

Decidophobia. The official term for being too scared

to make a decision. Maybe it's because you might upset or anger people – and receive death threats (like I have on several occasions). Seek support from your manager and discuss tough decisions with a mentor.

You don't know how. Follow your gut instincts. Failing that, create a matrix. On the horizontal axis, list all the factors that will influence your decision. On the vertical axis, list the options that are available to you. Score each individual option against each factor, and go with the option with the highest score.

You don't have time. Really, how much time does it take to make a decision? Get with the program. Remember, not making a decision is in itself making a decision.

#43 TECHNOLOGY BREAKDOWNS

Your screen freezes while you're working on a document you haven't saved. Your system crashes while you're on the phone to an impatient client. Your email server is down while your workload keeps piling up.

It's so ironic that technology, which has revolutionised productivity in every workplace, can also be a hindrance to the very productivity it created. When it's good, it's very good. But when it's bad, it fuels *technology rage*. It's just like road rage, only far more prolific. People will slam the keyboard, punch the screen, and curse at the hard drive, all with the aim of venting their frustrations.

Three main areas to be mindful of:

Help line. If your company has a help desk, it's, um, gotta be helpful. Questions like, 'Have you tried switching it off and turning it back on again?' are just plain insulting – although, I must admit, I've been guilty of neglecting this step.

Updated technology. As technology-savvy employees become more prevalent in the workplace, their preference will be to work for companies whose computer systems weren't in fashion at the same time as the Commodore 64. Your systems should be current and fast.

Take care. Have the latest anti-virus software installed, have a reliable back-up process in place that automatically stores data for easy retrieval, and provide employees with training on how to maintain their computers at optimum condition.

#42
IGNORING PROBLEMS

Sweeping issues under the carpet, pretending they don't exist, turning a blind eye. It's called the Ostrich Syndrome and it can make a complex life so much easier – in the short-term. Just ask Thabo Mbeki, the leader of South Africa, who for a decade was in denial that HIV led to AIDS. Today, one in ten South Africans are infected.

Or you can ask Kenneth Lay, of Enron fame, who oversaw the company's accounting irregularities, fraud, and corruption. It was convenient in the short-term. But in the long-term? Bankruptcy. International humiliation. 20,000 employees unemployed.

Or on a smaller scale, you can even ask me. When I'm driving my car and the engine begins to make unusual noises, I just turn the radio up louder. Problem solved – until, very recently, it went kaput in the middle of peak-hour traffic in a one-lane street.

The point I'm making is this: The avoidance of dealing with difficulties at work is tempting, but the consequences can be disastrous.

If your employees approach you with a problem, *listen*.

If you notice something that doesn't look right, *investigate*.

If you doubt an opinion that someone gives you, *analyse*.

If there's anything you don't clearly understand, *question*.

If you uncover suspicious behaviour, *shout*.

#41 OFFICE PSYCHOPATHS

I was the victim of a workplace bully for over two years. This psycho would say to me, 'I hate everything you say and everything you do.' He'd play pranks on staff members which would leave them crying. He'd fudge statistics, divulge secrets, and manipulate people to get what he wanted. He'd get promoted time and time again, charming his superiors, who didn't have a clue about the nightmare trail he was leaving behind.

You might have one of these psychopaths within your team, but you may not be aware of it because to your face they're polite, delightful, and high-achieving. But when you're not watching they become callous, vindictive, and controlling.

To *spot* an office psychopath, look out for these signs:

a short temper, little concern for others' feelings, impulsive emotions, no guilt over mistakes made, easily breaks the rules, the more-than-occasional lie, takes credit for others' work, and superficially conversational to important people.

To *deal* with office psychopaths, try these tips: sack them, sack them, sack them, sack them, sack them, sack them, sack them, sack them, sack them, sack them, sack them, sack them, sack them, sack them, sack them, sack them, sack them, sack them, and sack them.

It'd be easier to transform Eminem into an opera singer, George Bush into a unionist or Marilyn Manson into a kindergarten teacher than it would be to change the sinister inclinations of an office psychopath.

#40
DIRECTION AND GUIDANCE

Imagine the streets without road signs. Or the coastline without lighthouses. Or a person without a conscience. Drivers would never reach their destination, ships would crash against the rocks, and people would be cunning and evil. In each scenario: chaos.

Such is the value of a little direction and guidance – something which many workplaces are lacking. Notice I said *a little* – kinda like Michael Jackson's plastic surgery in the 80s as opposed to the work he had done in the 90s.

Our streets don't need to contain detailed steps for every destination, but a sign every hundred metres helps us stay on track. Our waters don't need a pole placed on every rock, but a lighthouse in the vicinity helps a lot.

People don't need to have every right and wrong spelt out for them, but a strong set of values keeps them decent.

The same principle applies at work. There's a big difference between *directing* and *direction*. *Directing* makes employees feel like they can't be trusted to use their own minds. *Direction* lets them know the parameters and foundation, which together guide them to where they need to be.

Think of a scale. On the left is *too little directing*, on the right is *too much directing*, and in the centre is *direction*. If you're offering *too little*, ramp up your communication and feedback. If it's *too much*, back off – give your employees room to learn, to make mistakes, and to deliver using their strengths.

#39
GOALS

If I hear one more management trainer or read one more management book that talks about SMART goals (*specific, measurable, adaptable, realistic, time-based*), I'm going to chuck a YouTube-worthy hissy fit. Alright already, we get it.

So I'm going to change it by introducing you to *DUMB* goals – *directed, unaware, many,* and *boring*. Goals can be as SMART as they come, but if they're interspersed with DUMBness, they're never going to work. So here are my big goal faux pas:

Directed. If goals are directed from the top down, there's very little chance your employees will embrace them. Your employees need to be part of the negotiations, or at the very least consulted with, before the goals are set.

Unaware. Many employees don't find out what their

goals are until many months into the new year. They need to have total clarity as soon as possible; like, in January. Goals also fail when there's no follow-up. Discuss their progress at least once a month.

Many. Sometimes we get carried away with setting too many goals. Managers who subscribe to the ridiculous theory of 'what gets measured gets done' are usually the main culprits. Narrow your goals down to no more than three. You'll find that if these three are achieved, they have flow-on effects to other areas.

Boring. Goals can be so uninspiring. Spice them up. Make them a challenge. Offer enticing rewards. Present them in colour. Introduce them with pizzazz. Display them on a funky wall. Make them fun and interesting so that they're memorable.

#38
BOREDOM

I recall a boring call centre job I once had. To keep myself entertained, I would play a game, where the aim was to eat food while I was on the phone to customers without them realising that I was eating. I'd start off easily with lollies, before slowly working up to harder foods like crackers that made loud crunching sounds while I ate them.

There was another job I had where I was so painfully bored that I would just send personal emails all day. On one day alone, I sent 146 emails to friends outside of work. Colleagues and managers would walk past my desk and when they saw me frantically typing away on the keyboard, they assumed I was *overworked*.

In many aspects of life there are techniques to stop us from being bored. For example, movies have twists, songs have hooks, and television shows have cliff-hangers. In the same way that creators of these genres engineer strategies to avoid consumer boredom, so must we with our employees.

Get busy. Employees with more work to do are more engaged than employees who don't have enough. Give employees additional responsibilities, autonomy, and opportunities to *solve* problems rather than to just *administer* them. Arouse their curiosity. Find out what stimulates them, excites them, and bring it on.

Get real. Scrap scripts – especially in call centres. Scripts create robotic and lifeless employees. Set your employees free to use their unique personalities to communicate with customers. Automate whatever is remotely repetitive. Be more *ideas*-driven rather than *process*-driven.

#37
FOCUSING ON THE BAD

People say that the world is getting worse, but I disagree. The world is getting *better* – it's more tolerant, open, and accessible than ever. It's just that *media coverage* is getting more extensive – and it's bad news that sells newspapers.

People who are beautiful will get one pimple and then lock themselves indoors thinking they're too ugly to be seen, while others with gorgeous bodies will put on an extra kilo and then consider themselves too fat to go to the beach. As a society, we focus so much on what isn't right about our lives instead of marvelling over the magnificent. (Come to think of it, this book is a case in point!) We'll analyse our inadequacies instead of making the most of our abilities. And to paraphrase Malcolm Forbes, *we undervalue what we have and overvalue what we don't.*

This especially occurs at work. We'll focus more on employees' mistakes than on their achievements. We'll communicate bad news more than we communicate good news. We'll discipline our staff more than we recognise them. We'll have more crisis meetings than we have achievement meetings. We'll try to control more than we set free.

If more than half of what you say to your team is of a negative nature, then you're guilty. There shouldn't be a balance between positivity and negativity at work. There's got to be an *imbalance* in favour of positivity.

#36
HYPOCRISY

We're surrounded by hypocrisy everywhere we look. Political extremists aggressively campaign against gay rights but then get caught having homosexual affairs. Athletes appear in 'just say no to drugs' advertisements but then get busted taking steroids. Religious fundamentalists go on moral crusades and then father illegitimate children.

So it's really not surprising that hypocrisy is endemic in the working world as well. We'll announce a crackdown on lateness – but then take long lunches ourselves. We'll cut staffing budgets – but then increase executive salaries. We'll ask employees to offer outstanding customer service – but then treat them like disposable toiletries.

I'm not suggesting that workplace hypocrites intentionally go out of their way to be hypocritical. The majority wouldn't even realise they're behaving that way.

There really isn't a 7-step process, a magic formula, or an academic model to help a hypocrite stop being a hypocrite. The solution is simply to ... stop being a hypocrite. It's pretty easy. But I guess before someone can *stop* doing anything, they've first got to *spot* their hypocritical behaviours. *Spot before you stop*, so to speak.

You're a hypocrite if 'do as I say, not do as I do' is your thing. You're a hypocrite if you say things like 'just this one time'. You're a hypocrite if you think you can play by different rules ... just because you're a manager.

#35 WASTED TALENTS

Imagine Leonardo da Vinci if he wasn't allowed to paint. Or JK Rowling if she was prohibited from writing. Or Madonna if she was prevented from acting...

These extraordinary talents would have lain dormant and the world would have been at a loss. The same scenario occurs at work.

The biggest driver of job satisfaction is to identify each employee's unique talents and find some way, *any way*, to incorporate them into their role. Unfortunately, most employees come to work and follow a standard routine without having any opportunity to put into practice the passions that excite them.

I'm not saying your employees' talents should *become* their work; rather, you can transform your employees' levels of engagement just by utilising their natural talents in some capacity while they're working for you – even if it's just for an hour or two a week.

A creative person in an Accounts team might redesign the invoices. A numbers person in a call centre might analyse metrics and reporting. A social person might be responsible for enhancing inter-departmental relationships.

Whatever it is, if you feel your employees aren't satisfied with their jobs, it's probably because their talents are being wasted.

#34 TAKING CREDIT FOR OTHERS' WORK

It really is armed robbery of a different kind, isn't it? You're armed with power and you're robbing intellectual property. It's not indictable, but it's indecent. It's not unforgivable, but it's unfair. It's not Al Capone, but it's Winona Ryder.

Managers who take the credit for their employees' work reminds me of a scene in *Grease* where Sandy (played by Olivia Newton-John) squeals at Danny (played by John Travolta): 'You're a fake and a phoney and I wish I never laid eyes on you!'

You might think it's harmless (like Winona Ryder's shoplifting), but to the people who've missed out on getting credit for their ideas, you might be stealing something they've poured their heart and soul into; you might be stealing work they've laboured over for years. In many instances, that's worse than stealing their purse or television.

According to the *National Association for Shoplifting Prevention*, only 3 per cent of shoplifters steal because they're short of money. The majority steal because of the *high* they feel once they get away with it.

If you're a Credit Lifter at work, you're obviously going after the same kind of high, such as the high of recognition or the high of being promoted. Just know you'd get an even bigger high when you become known as a manager that talented people *love* working for simply because you inspire them to be their best. That's when you'll really get noticed – and experience the most intense highs of all.

#33 CONSTANT CHANGES

Employees are not against change. In fact, they love it. They embrace changes in fashion before a garment's been worn three times; they purchase new technology before the old gadget's batteries have run out; and they download new music before they've had a chance to get over what they heard last week.

Nope, employees are not against change. The only reason they're against change in the workplace is because it's frequently implemented badly. After being burned a few times, of course they're going to become cynical.

For employees to be engaged during any workplace change, three factors must be met: *consultation, involvement,* and *advocacy.*

Consult. Before any change is implemented, meet

with your employees to let them know. Use this as an opportunity to seek their feedback, to get their thoughts on how the change will affect them, and to encourage ideas on how the change can be effective.

Involve. Employees accept change more readily when they've played a part in its implementation. Develop a few employees into subject-matter experts, get others involved in testing, and engage some in a post-implementation review.

Advocate. Let employees know how the change will benefit *them* and why it's better than the status quo. Work on converting a few of your most influential team members into fans, which will make it easier for others to follow their lead. And celebrate your key milestones and successes.

#32 PAY AND REWARDS

It's amazing that out of 2,400 respondents, pay and rewards only managed to make it to number 32 on this list. And to even get it to that ranking, I had to combine *all* monetary-related responses, such as commissions, incentives, and bonuses. This implies that pay and rewards are important – just not *that* important.

So here's what this means for you. If you suck at managing, or if your jobs are more painful than a hernia, or if your workplace conditions are akin to a North Korean labour camp, then you'd better be paying twice as much as your competitors. For everyone else, the magic number is *20 per cent more*.

To remain competitive in a tight employment market, you have to be paying your best employees 20 per cent more than what they could possibly be earning with your competitors.

But here's the twist: the extra 20 per cent doesn't need to just be financial. It can be a combination of extrinsic factors (such as cash, gifts, and discounts), as well as *intrinsic* elements such as career opportunities, job enrichment, workplace relationships, learning development, and work/life balance.

So long as your employees know that they're getting 20 per cent more value from you than they could get from any other potential employer, money won't be an issue for you.

#31 RUDENESS AND UNFRIENDLINESS

I'd like to introduce you to my ex-manager – 'The Dragon'. She'd never smile, she'd avoid interacting with us, and she'd yell 'NOT NOW, JAMES' as I'd walk to her desk to ask her a question. Unsurprisingly, all of us despised working for her.

She was rude, unfriendly, and stank of self-importance. And if you think that management is *not* a popularity contest, think again. If you're popular there's a far greater chance people will want to do more for you.

One day, The Dragon must have received some feedback from her manager that she was a cow because she miraculously started to smile. But it was a forced, stretched, uncomfortable smile. She thought the act of smiling simply involved showing us her teeth. It didn't make us feel better; it gave us the creeps. My advice: *smile genuinely*.

Be happy to be where you are – or get the hell out.

The Dragon would act as if we didn't exist. I sat literally one metre away from her, and I would get changed from my work clothes into my gym gear – *right in front of her* – and she wouldn't even notice. My advice: say hello, be interested in the people working for you, get to know them, and have relaxed conversations.

When The Dragon did talk to us, it was only when she had something negative to say. My advice: for every negative comment that comes out of your mouth, have two wonderful things to say. It makes people enjoy the time they spend with you.

#30 PROCESS VIOLATIONS

Chances are you've got a bunch of metaphorical left-brain thinkers who love logic, analysis, and objectivity. Their linear thinking makes them sensitive to flaws. They adore models and rationality. Processes work well with these guys.

So you can imagine their frustration when they see their right-brained colleagues bending the rules, cutting corners, and skipping important steps. It makes them as angry as a feminist in the '60s. That is, the 1860s.

To deal with process violators, we've first got to establish why they're breaking the rules.

There's a better way. Your processes are archaic. They're there because ... well, just because. People break them because they're so annoying. *Solution:* Update your processes. Scrap those that are unnecessary and shorten the ones that are tragically long.

They're over it. They're exhausted, lethargic, and bored. They've lost interest in their work. They're no longer motivated to do a great job. *Solution:* Give them more interesting work to do and stimulate them with new challenges.

They're not aware. Your processes aren't clear, or they're too complicated. Or maybe your employees don't even know what they are. *Solution:* Document your processes and have them easily accessible. Provide regular training, coaching, and refresher updates.

They're indifferent. Some employees simply don't care. They don't derive meaning or value from their work – or *any* work for that matter. They're just plain lazy and think that work is for suckers. *Solution:* Free them up to explore opportunities outside of the organisation.

#29
MERITOCRACY

At the time of writing, the ten poorest countries in the world (as measured by GDP per capita) do not have recognised democracies in place. Out of the ten richest countries, *six* have fully-fledged democratic governments operating.

This statistic indicates that autocracies, usually ruled by a power-hungry dictator, have a disastrous effect on people's lives. Rarely are dictators elevated to positions of authority because of their talents. It's usually because of their family connections, race, wealth, or military power. The saddening economic and social consequences speak for themselves.

And so it is at work. When people are promoted not because of merit, achievements and skills, but because of influential connections, longevity and cronyism, the consequence is chaos.

When deciding who to promote, there should be one question on your mind only: *Which person will excel the most in this role?* To promote someone based on any other factor sets you up for failure. And the unsuccessful internal candidates should be placed on comprehensive career development programs to help them reach the required level.

It's just like in the episode of *The Simpsons* where Homer gets promoted just because he has hair all of a sudden. Chaos ensues, but the ever-oblivious Homer retorts: 'I think Smithers picked me because of my motivational skills. Everyone says they have to work a lot harder when I'm around.' The result? Homer was fired.

#28
BUREAUCRACY

Oh, it's such an ugly word. Ugly, ugly, ugly. Bureaucracy is the enemy of employee engagement. If it were the Wicked Witch of the West, it would take a bucketful of engagement strategies to melt it away.

And yet companies are mired in forms and paperwork and processes and levels of authority, and all of it in the name of consistency, when all bureaucracy ever produces is complacency, constriction, and 'I-can't-stand-this-anymore' cries for help.

Bureaucracy punishes the many for the stupidity of the few. It imposes strict rules and guidelines which serve to strangle daring and exciting thinking. Like an unsightly mole, it grows bigger and bigger with every new management strategy until eventually no-one has a clue which procedure to follow ... they just know they're meant to be following *some* kind of procedure.

Push approvals all the way down. And I'm talkin' *way* down. Give employees more authority to make decisions without always having to seek the okay. Let them solve customer problems, even ones that require a financial solution.

Conduct a review that focuses solely on the scrapping of unnecessary systems and protocols – a review that aims to eliminate paper, cut time wastage, and remove blockages to productivity.

Mary Mary sang it beautifully in their hit song when they referred to the shackles that weighed them down. Sure, the song was really all about praising Jesus, but come to think of it, the most bureaucratic of companies require a divine intervention.

#27 OVERWORKED

Hard work never killed anybody, but why take a chance?
Edgar Bergen

By working faithfully eight hours a day, you may get to be a boss and work twelve hours a day.
Robert Frost

In an environment where companies are focusing increasingly on shareholder value, employees are being squeezed to do more with less. On the positive side, it's a good idea to run lean and efficient businesses. But on the negative side, if employees are being swamped with too much work, it easily leads to stress, absenteeism, and burnout.

Encourage a work/life balance. The best way to encourage a work/life balance is to have one yourself. Be the example. Other ways can include clamping down on employees who work long hours and being flexible with their needs outside of work.

Run efficient meetings. Most meetings are a waste of time. Make them efficient by inviting only people who really *should* be there; follow an agenda; stop off-track conversations; and keep all meetings running on time.

Negotiate deadlines. Don't *impose* deadlines – negotiate them. Ask your employees for what they feel is a suitable turnaround time. If their response doesn't suit the workplace demand, see what other parts of their workload can be rearranged.

Enforce breaks. If you notice employees skipping breaks, having shorter lunches, or eating at their desks, take a stand. Get employees to go out of the office for some fresh air.

#26 DESPERATELY SEEKING SUPPORT

Once upon a time, three little pigs built three houses: one made of straw, another made of wood, and a third made from bricks.

One day a wolf went to the straw house. 'Little pig, little pig, let me come in,' he growled. 'Not by the hair on my chinny chin chin,' answered the pig. 'Then I'll huff and I'll puff and I'll blow your house down.' So the wolf huffed and he puffed and he blew the house down, so the pig ran to the wooden house.

The wolf followed. 'Little pigs, little pigs, let me come in,' bellowed the wolf. 'Not by the hair on our chinny chin chins,' cried the pigs. 'Then I'll huff and I'll puff and I'll blow your house down.' So he huffed and he puffed and he blew the wooden house down, so the two pigs ran to the third pig's house.

The wolf then proceeded to the brick house. 'Little pigs, little pigs, let me come in,' snarled the wolf. 'Not by the hair on our chinny chin chins,' shouted the pigs. 'Then I'll huff and I'll puff and I'll blow your house down.' So the wolf huffed and he puffed but he *couldn't* blow the brick house down. It was too strong.

Moral of the fairytale: The support you're providing your employees is made of straw, wood, or bricks. To provide strong, brick-solid support, have frequent catch-ups, regular coaching, lend a hand, provide required resources, encourage breaks, and understand their needs.

#25 INCOMPETENT MANAGEMENT

Some people aspire to be managers for all the wrong reasons, even when their people skills show they'd be more suited to something more remote, like lighthouse keeping. In this quiz, give yourself a rating out of 5 for each statement. Zero means you've *never* committed the offence, and 5 means that you always do it.

- You delegate work without considering employee workloads: ___
- You don't think you should explain your decisions: ___
- You focus more on small tasks rather than the big picture: ___
- You haven't delivered one-on-one coaching in a long time: ___

- You find yourself managing more crises than initiating ideas: ___
- You believe that mistakes are unacceptable and punish them: ___
- You promote your personal favourites over the best candidates: ___
- You deliver negative feedback to employees in front of others: ___
- You haven't had a recent work/life balance discussion: ___
- You talk more than you listen: ___
- You have a greater focus on your employees' faults: ___
- You're not always honest with your employees: ___
- You participate in office gossip: ___
- You've broken promises to one or more employees: ___
- You don't feel your employees should provide you with feedback: ___
- You don't provide your employees with recognition every day: ___
- You don't clearly understand your employees' expectations: ___
- You believe it's unnecessary to build close employee relationships: ___
- You don't know what your employees' natural talents are: ___

If you obtained a total of more than 20, you might be deficient in the biggest driver of managerial success: *emotional intelligence*. Read this book twice.

#24
INPUT AND CONSULTATION

Imagine this scenario. Your husband or wife announces one day that the whole family is moving to a smaller house in a suburb further away and less safe. No discussion, no explanation, and no warning. If that were me, I'd be rehearsing for the next season of *The Bachelor* before my bags had even been packed.

A similar scenario plays out in the workplace. Change is forced upon employees without their input or consultation. It's not about seeking your employees' *permission*. It's simply giving them the opportunity to *influence* what's going on.

It comes down to this: *employees just want to have a say in changes that are going to affect them.*

Here are some questions you can ask during a consultation phase:

- This is what we're planning – how do you think it'll affect you?
- How can we implement this more effectively?
- Can you foresee any challenges in making this work?
- Do you think this is a good idea? Why, or why not?

And if you're going to seek your employees' input, you've got to do it with sincerity. For example, Hollywood producer Samuel Goldwyn once remarked: 'I don't want any yes-men around me. I want everyone to tell me the truth – even if it costs them their jobs.'

#23
EXPECTATIONS

Work can be just like internet dating. Allow me to explain.

When you meet someone new online, expectations begin to form. Initially these are *explicit* expectations. This is the stuff people specifically tell you, such as where they live, what they do for work, and whether or not they have teeth. When you get together in person and you see they seem nothing at all like they'd described, expectations are broken, and there's rarely ever a second date.

Managers do a similar thing at work. We set explicit expectations by what we say, such as advocating career opportunities, promising training, pledging salary increases, and so on. The moment just one of these is unmet, trust is broken, and there's rarely ever a second chance.

Even more dangerous than explicit expectations are the *implicit* ones. These are the expectations that people form without us even having to say *a single thing*. In the online dating world, these can include your potential partner dreamily imagining your wedding day – before you've even exchanged phone numbers.

At work, employees form implicit expectations such as what their job will be like, the type of manager they'll have, the colleagues they'll be working with, and so on. And just like explicit expectations, break one of these and you're screwed.

The solution is to continuously have up-front, honest conversations so that you always know precisely what your employees are thinking and expecting. Expectations can only be managed once you know what they are. Watch what you promise.

#22
OFFICE POLITICS

I recall being passed over for a promotion once, and the only feedback I received from the senior executive was that I wasn't 'aware of office politics'. She even recommended a book on the subject.

Office politics is like spam – intrusive, irritating, and here to stay. It's a fact of life in every company. You can try to clamp down on it as much as you can but you'll exhaust yourself trying to do so. The solution is to try to manage it so that it's not so destructive. Here's how.

Explain. Articulate why you do what you do. When you make a big decision, explain your reasoning. When you promote someone, share the reasons why the successful person got the job.

Don't join in. Choosing sides, participating in gossip,

and accepting favours must be scratched off your to-do list.

Communicate. Rumour is fuelled by secrets and stifled by open communication. Be transparent, listen to employee concerns, and be impartial.

Unmet needs. Generally, office politics is inflamed by the insecurities of your employees. Identify their unmet needs (such as recognition, career development, and job satisfaction) that may be driving your employees to buy in to office politics.

#21
DISRESPECT

The tricky thing about showing employees that we respect them is that 'respect' means different things to different people. To some employees, respect might be the amount of attention we give them, while to others respect might be shown in the amount of time we leave them alone. But there are some universal laws that govern respect.

Make people feel important. Greet your employees with enthusiasm and energy. Surprise them with a small gift that makes them say 'wow'.

Show interest. If you don't know your employees' histories, ambitions, partners' names, kids' names, hobbies, likes, and dislikes, you're about as interested as a nun at a speed-dating night.

Be grateful. As children, one of the first terms we're

taught to say is 'thank you' – yet as we get older it seems to escape our vocabulary. Sincerely express your gratitude.

Trust them. Stretch people with responsibilities and projects that may seem beyond their capabilities. Don't over-supervise them.

Connect. Focus on what people are saying. Use open body language. Eliminate distractions. Refer to previous conversations later on to show you value what they said.

The better you know your employees and the stronger your relationships with them, the easier it'll be for you to figure out precisely what constitutes respect in their mind.

#20
LISTENING

You might have had someone squeal at you in the past, usually in a fit of rage, 'You're listening to me but you're not *hearing* me!' (Or is it, 'You're hearing me but you're not *listening* to me'?) Whatever it is, it seems many of us are better at talking than listening. You've got to become a master at listening – otherwise your employees will feel like unwanted stepchildren. There are four main ways to do this:

Reserve judgement. Before deciding whether your employee's idea is good or bad, first hear it out. If you make a judgement too early, especially a negative one, your body language will show you've switched off. Let them finish talking.

Focus on content. It's hard to get past a bad communicator, but within that painful delivery may be a nugget of gold. Pretend you're Oprah and that your job is to listen carefully to everything your interviewee says.

Be present. If eye contact freaks you out, try looking at the bridge of the nose or on the lower forehead, and it won't be so freaky. Add to the mix the occasional nod and the perfectly timed *hmmms* and *aaahs*, and you're almost there. If you're easily distracted, perhaps conduct your listening in private rooms or quiet areas.

Ask questions. Show that you genuinely care about what's being said by asking a few questions. Maybe even take notes and refer to the conversation at a later date.

#19 DISMISSING IDEAS

The word 'no' is such a powerful word. It can make some people cry, make others defiant, and it can fuel a whole range of negative emotions. Dismissing employees' ideas before you've heard them in full – or even before you've given them a chance to work – stifles innovation and creativity.

You haven't got all the answers. World-renowned products like the Big Mac and Google Adwords were the creative genius of lowly employees who had managers embracing their ideas rather than blocking them.

Set goals for innovation. Provide incentives to encourage your team to come up with new ideas. I bet they'll come up with better concepts in a few minutes than your entire leadership team at a five-day retreat.

Reward risk-takers. There's a major difference between being a *risk taker* and being *risky*. In a world that's undergoing change at a faster rate than ever before, it's the most outrageous thinkers who'll prosper.

Listen more. If you find yourself talking more than listening, and telling more than asking, take a deep breath. And hold it.

Seek suggestions. Actively ask employees for their thoughts on what can be improved, changed, added, and removed. 'Suggestion boxes' don't count. Do it in person.

Consider. Before responding to an employee's idea, stop. Hold the pause. Think about whether what you're about to say is going to equate to a 'talk to the hand because the ears ain't listening' – and then rephrase.

#18
PERSONAL PERFORMANCE

Some employees look no further than themselves for their lacklustre performance. When they compare themselves to their colleagues or they receive a disappointing performance review, they feel like the Miss Teen South Carolina contestant who was asked why one-fifth of Americans can't locate the US on a map. Her response:

'I personally believe that US Americans are unable to do so because some people out there in our nation don't have maps, and I believe that our education, like such as South Africa and the Iraq, everywhere like, such as, and I believe that they should, our education over here in the US, should help the US, err, should help South Africa and should help the Iraq and the Asian countries, so we will be able to build up our future for our children.'

There are four main reasons why employees don't perform:

Don't know. They haven't got a clue how to do the work, so spend some time with them focusing on the *'how'* rather than just the *'what'*.

Don't care. The employees can do the work, but simply don't want to. The solution is to find out why. Ask great open-ended questions.

Could not. External barriers (out of their control) are impeding their success. Poor ergonomics might be the cause or really restrictive procedures.

Could never. They don't have the skills and abilities to ever do the job. Place them in a new role that's more suited to their strengths and review your recruitment process.

#17
MICROMANAGEMENT

I'll never forget the chilling scene in *Silence of the Lambs* when Hannibal Lecter is strapped to a trolley, his upper body encased in a constricting white straitjacket – unable to move, not even an inch. Attached to his face is a tight hockey mask. Just by watching it, the viewer can't help but feel suffocated.

And yet millions of employees around the world are subjected to the same kind of thing. Instead of a straitjacket, it's archaic and unbreakable policies that restrict creativity and freedom to think. And instead of a hockey mask, it's overbearing managers breathing down their employees' necks, watching their every move like prison guards.

Micromanagement is making your experienced employees feel like children, and your talented employees feel dumber than a goldfish. Micromanagers are control freaks. They complain that 'young kids these days have no work ethic' – without giving them a chance to develop one. They'll say 'I could do it better myself', and tragically refrain from delegating.

Allow people to make mistakes without punishing them for it. Only ever punish inaction. Share information so that employees can take responsibility. Give people projects to lead, training sessions to run, and room to make their own decisions. Let go of the reins.

Hannibal Lecter said it best to Jodie Foster's character: 'Given the chance, you would deny me my life, wouldn't you?' No, not your life, replies Foster. Hannibal retorts: 'Just my freedom. You'd take that from me.'

#16
INFORMATION UNDERLOAD

It's ironic that we're living in the *Information Age* and yet so many employees are complaining that they're not receiving enough information. It's as crazy as a jury without evidence or a surgeon without an X-ray.

The common information infringements of which you or your company may be culpable include:

Withholding. This applies to those who live by the term 'on a need-to-know basis'. If you know something, share it. Let your employees decide what they 'need to know'. If you learn something from senior management, cascade it to your team. 'Information *overload*' didn't even appear *once* in this entire 2,400-person study.

Spinning. Like desperate defence lawyers who twist and turn information to suit their needs, you might be doing the exact same thing. Just be honest. Going through a restructure? Tell it like it is. Bad press coverage? Tell it like it is. Any challenges ahead? Just tell it like it is.

Lacking. Occasionally, it's not that information is manipulated or withheld; it's just that it's not *there*. And employees end up wasting valuable time trying to find it. So make it easy to access. Have an online directory where you store this stuff, or a manual that gets updated regularly, or people that are readily available to help.

So, flaunt it. Work it. Come out of the closet and tell people what they need to know.

#15
BLAME

There are three kinds of people in the workplace: Heart Souls, Mind Souls, and Arse Souls.

Heart Souls. If you're this kind of person, you rock. You believe that no matter what happens to you, no-one else is to blame. You look no further than yourself to see how your thoughts, actions, and behaviour have contributed to every situation. You live by the Zig Ziglar maxim that 'when you point the finger at someone else, you've got three fingers pointing right back at you'. You'll go far in life and people will love you.

Mind Souls. If this is you, you're happy to take the blame, but only if you feel it's not going to land you in hot water. If it seems as though by accepting blame you'll look like a team player, you'll do it. But if it's going to jeopardise your career or reputation, you'll spread that blame around like a bad cold.

Arse Souls. If you're this person, you refuse to take blame and relish in apportioning it. You're the equivalent of a pathological liar. You actually *believe* that others are always to blame. You're the kind of person who'd blame the government's handling of the economy for your poor financial situation, even though you don't learn about money. You're the type of person who would blame your manager for your work dissatisfaction without seeing how your attitude causes the problem. You whinge and complain, you drain people of their positive energy, and you're boring. You need help.

#14
DISHONESTY

- *I value your opinion.* Unless it makes me look bad...
- *Our employees are our greatest asset.* But if you quit, you quit...
- *I won't tell you how to do your job.* Except when I have a better way...
- *No-one's getting a bonus this year.* Except for executives...
- *We always advertise internal vacancies.* After we already know who we're promoting...

Lies, lies, lies. Sometimes they're innocent white lies like 'we're still thinking it over' when a decision has already been made, and at other times they're downright outrageous lies like 'we offer flexible working conditions', which means if *you're* not flexible with *our* conditions, you're out.

If there's one thing that really upsets people, it's dishonesty. Marriages have been broken, friendships have been shattered, and business partnerships have been dissolved – all because someone told a lie, and then another, and then another ... And therein lies the problem with dishonesty – it becomes a habit.

Admit it. Whenever you lie, go back and confess. Apologise for your actions. Holding yourself accountable will compel you to tell the truth moving forward.

Make a list. Keep track of each time you lie and the reason why. You'll notice a trend of the types of situations you should avoid.

Reward yourself. If you start to lie less and less, treat yourself with a reward and continue to do so until you're no longer a big fat liar.

#13 BROKEN PROMISES

You say you will, but then you don't
You think that I won't see
You build me up, then bring me down
Get real, you can't fool me

You raise my hopes by talking big
You think that I'm naïve
When really all your talk is cheap
Get lost, I don't believe

You're killing our relationship
Each time you let me down
Each time you break a promise
And each time you say 'not now'

I've learned now not to trust you
I've been burned too many times
Your habit's too familiar
I can see through your disguise

It's time for me to say goodbye
There's a better boss I'll pick
I'll move on, I'll be just fine
But you'll still be a …

#12
FAVOURITISM

It's almost as bad as having a favourite child, isn't it? One of my favourite comedians, Fiona O'Loughlin, says that if your parents ever tell you they don't have a favourite child, that's because ... it isn't you.

I think it's perfectly natural for managers to have favourite employees. I once turned a blind eye when an employee threw a computer on the floor simply because I found him so adorable. I've learned since then.

Whether it's your best performer, or the one who never calls in sick, or the one who makes you laugh the most, you wouldn't be human if you didn't gravitate towards one or two of your employees. But here's what brilliant managers know. There's a big difference between *having* favourites and *playing* favourites.

Playing favourites means spending most of your time hanging out with one or two employees. *Having* favourites means *wanting* to spend more time with certain employees but consciously spreading your attention amongst the team.

Playing favourites means promoting someone to a higher position simply because you like them the most. *Having* favourites means *wishing* you could promote your buddy up the corporate ladder, but being smart enough to promote the best person instead.

Playing favourites means being harder on those in the team you don't get along with that well. *Having* favourites means abiding by a fair system of evaluation that applies to everyone – no matter how high they are on your social hierarchy.

#11
CONDESCENDING & DICTATORIAL MANAGERS

If there were ever an organisation that worships authority, rules by force, and uses intimidating tactics, it would have to be the Mafia, which has inspired many managers to adopt similar Mafioso methods at work. Several years ago, when Sicilian police arrested a major Godfather, they discovered the 'Mafia Ten Commandments' – a guide to being a decent gangster. I've paraphrased them here with my workplace interpretation in italics.

- **All introductions must be through a third party.** *Be careful with whom you associate. Collaborate with positive and genuinely good people.*
- **Never look at the wives of friends.** *Be loyal. It tends to be reciprocated.*

- **Never be seen with cops.** *Whose side are you on? Work with your employees, not against them.*
- **Don't go to pubs and clubs.** *Always be present, be coherent, and be real.*
- **Always be available for duty – even if your wife's giving birth.** *Be there for your employees and provide unshakeable support.*
- **Respect appointments.** *Your employees' time is just as important as yours.*
- **Treat wives with respect.** *Don't talk down to people. Be polite and courteous.*
- **Always tell the truth.** *Don't hide, deceive, or mislead.*
- **Money can't be stolen from other families.** *Be fair. Don't do to others what you'd hate done to you.*
- **People to be excluded: anyone who behaves badly and doesn't have moral values.** *If being condescending and authoritative is a habit you can't break, perhaps management is a profession from which you should be excluded.*

#10 DEADLINES AND TIME

Harry Houdini had a famous escape – the Chinese Water Torture Cell. His legs would be locked in stocks, his body would be lowered upside-down into a tank overflowing with water, and then finally a metal cage would be added to prevent him from turning within the cell. It was then up to Houdini to escape ... while holding his breath for three minutes.

What a deadline ... and by the way some employees react to deadlines, you'd think they had time management issues as pressing as Houdini's. And yet you should still ...

Monitor workloads. Check with your employees occasionally to make sure they haven't taken on too much work. They might have trouble saying 'no'.

Clarify responsibilities. Perhaps your employees' time is being taken up with tasks they shouldn't be doing.

Be clear on what they are and aren't meant to do.

Supply resources. Employees may struggle if they haven't got access to the tools and people they need to perform. Ask them what's missing and make it available.

Provide training. Your employees might need to brush up on their skills, so send them on a course. (Although I once attended a program on 'Time Management' during which I asked the facilitator what time we'd be finishing. He replied, '4:30, maybe 5 o'clock. It depends on how long it'll take me to get through the material.' Riiight.)

#9
GOSSIP AND BACKSTABBING

You didn't hear this from me, but I reckon the best TV show ever made would have to be *Melrose Place*. Okay, it did lose some credibility the second time Kimberley died, but the bitchiness and backstabbing was irresistible. It screened on Australian TV on Tuesday nights, and I remember on Wednesday mornings it was all we could talk about in the office.

So what is it about salacious gossip and raunchy rumour that makes us drop everything, walk straight to the water cooler, and indulge in a whispering conversation about other people's dirty laundry? Oh, I know. *It's so much fun*. Until *we* become the subject of the latest titillating tittle-tattle.

Gossip, rumour, bitchiness, backstabbing – it's all impossible to eliminate. But it's destructive. Productivity suffers. Morale takes a hit. Cliques begin to form. And so we've got to minimise it as much as possible. My two cents' worth:

Cent #1 – Opt out. First and foremost, no matter how tempting, refrain from being part of the gossip. This is especially difficult during after-work drinks or the staff Christmas party – both occasions when your relaxed state of mind makes you feel like opening up.

Cent #2 – Crack down. Don't tolerate any of this at work. If you see it in action, speak to the people involved. Treat the spreading of rumours and office bitchiness in the same way you'd respond to someone who makes a racially discriminatory comment.

#8
TEAM? WHAT TEAM?

When I was at university, I hated group assignments. And I mean I *seriously* hated them. I'm not even an introvert, and yet giving birth to a lawnmower would have been preferable to working with others on a group project. (At least, I imagine it would be.)

And I know I'm in the majority. Group assignments sucked, and let's face it, work is really just one big group assignment.

So it's not surprising that *lack of teamwork* has appeared at number eight in this study. People who barely know each other – heck, barely even *like* each other – are placed into teams and expected to perform. And when they don't, here's what amuses me the most: *we run team-building sessions*, hoping that the playing of childish and mindless games will result in team cohesion and effectiveness.

So here's the big secret: you can't create teamwork. You just can't. It's not a noun. It's not a thing. You can't make it, develop it, create it, or formulate it. All you can do is set up the right kind of environment so that teamwork just ... happens. The environment you need to set up consists of:

Air. Give employees opportunities to express their opinions and ideas.

Animals. Make sure all employees are clear on each others' roles and responsibilities.

Land. Have a strong foundation in place with solid team processes.

Water. Monitor communication channels so that they're always free-flowing.

Sun. Ensure there's understanding of the team's goals, purpose, and reason for existence.

#7 ANNOYING AND INCONSIDERATE CO-WORKERS

Filthy coffee mugs left in the kitchen sink. Bathroom hygiene resembling a dirty bomb. Colleagues with offensive body odour. People who just want to chitchat casually while others are swamped with work. Loud and obnoxious employees in the office. The use of electronic devices during meetings. Employees stealing their colleagues' stationery.

All of these – *and then some* – are the most common annoying characteristics that employees tolerate from the people they work with. You can run as many team-building days as you like – but your annoying employees will still be despised by their colleagues.

In order of effectiveness:

Address it. It's time to have a difficult conversation. Raise the issue one-on-one with the offending employee.

Be gentle, but don't beat around the bush. Link the irritating behaviour with the impact it has on the business.

Undress it. Take action to prevent the annoying behaviours from occurring in the first place. For example, at the beginning of meetings ask that all electronic devices are turned off; run weekly stationery audits so that employees can stock up on supplies; place complimentary toiletries in the bathrooms; and so on.

Redress it. This is where you deal with the annoying behaviour by getting *everyone* to do it so that it becomes the norm. You might encourage everyone to leave their dirty mugs in the kitchen sink (and then set up a kitchen-cleaning roster or hire a cleaner); you might encourage everyone to be chatty and loud (and only hire people that love it), etc.

#6
CUSTOMERS

Let's get real for a second. The customer is *not* always right. In many cases, they're annoying, demanding, and just plain stupid. I know this for a fact, having worked in call centres and retail for a long time, and of course, being a customer myself, I readily admit to being annoying, demanding, and just plain stupid plenty of times.

So here's the deal. The more you passionately shout from the rooftops that the 'customer is always right', that the customer is your 'number one asset', and other such fallacies, the more your employees will think you're an idiot. Scrap such sayings from your vocabulary, trash the posters in your workplace that profess these inaccuracies, and start doing three important things.

Firstly, relate to your employees. If they approach you

with a gripe about a particular customer or you receive a customer complaint, consider taking your employee's side. Or at least hear them out first.

Secondly, sack your customers. Quite frankly, some of them are bad for your business. If you've got a handful of customers that make work a living hell for your employees, get rid of them before your employees decide to leave instead.

And thirdly, figure out what your customers are doing that's making your employees' blood pressure rise, and then do something about each of those things. It might not necessarily be faults with your customers or faults with your employees, but faults with your systems.

#5
NEGATIVITY

The biggest killer of people today is *negativity*. Of course, I haven't a skerrick of evidence to back up my claim, but I'd bet my first-born child that I'm right. Like a contagious disease, negative employees infect everyone with their poison.

They complain and whinge and moan and whine. Of course, this isn't just limited to your employees. You could be guilty of being a negativity breeder yourself.

If it's you. When times are tough, that's when you need to be extra positive. Any negativity you exert, whether it's in the words you use, the body language you display, or the decisions you make, will impact your team like a slap in the face. The first slap might not hurt so much, but the second or third really start to sting. When you feel yourself becoming negative, go for a walk, read a motivational quote, breathe, or find a joke to laugh about.

If it's someone in your team. Provide feedback by focusing on their actions (not their personality) and the impact they're having on others. Maybe they need a job change, a new project, or a new employer. If negative employees express a problem, ask them for the solution rather than trying to solve it yourself. Role model the behaviour you most want to see, offer praise and recognition when warranted, and use positive language.

#4 ACCOUNTABILITY AND RESPONSIBILITY

It's so common to see words being used interchangeably when they're really quite different. Words like *belief* and *faith*, *dream* and *goal*, *want* and *need* are a few examples. I also love hearing oxymorons. A few of my favourites are *open relationship*, *healthy tan*, and *working holiday*.

Two words which fall victim to false interchanges and oxymorons are *accountability* and *responsibility*. Firstly, they have different meanings. And secondly, you can't be *partly responsible* or *jointly accountable*. You're either responsible – or you're not. And you're either accountable – or you're not. There's no in between. To imply otherwise is like saying you're only partly human or jointly Chinese.

And so it is that a lack of responsibility and a shortfall

of accountability are two of the biggest drivers of employee angst in the workplace.

You *promote* responsibility by giving employees the training and resources they need to perform, and you *assign* accountability when you make sure that one individual is liable for the consequences of a process, project, or goal. *Managing accountability* is a management responsibility. Get it?

I'll give you another example. My dear friend, Al Fresco (not his real name), has a relative who was recently arrested for possessing drugs. His relative was ultimately *responsible* for the actions that led to the arrest and is now being held *accountable* for the ramifications.

Be clear on the distinction, enforce it, and you'll avoid any nasty finger-pointing.

#3 COMMUNICATION ISSUES

I once ran a communications audit for a large multinational, and I recall a lady remarking during a focus group: 'My manager sits 30 metres away from me and he sends me documents through *internal mail*.' They clearly had serious issues.

Be first. The rule here is: *No surprises.* Your employees should find out important information from you – not through the grapevine or after it's happened.

Be real. Don't hide behind email. It's the least effective way of engaging your employees. Interact face-to-face as much as possible.

Be tuned. Communication is a *two-way* process. This means that what you *hear* is often more important than what you *say*. I've got a friend who gets so entranced by her own voice that she can't even hear me when I interject.

She doesn't check at all for my response. I'll put the phone down, go to the bathroom, and come back a few minutes later – and she's still rambling.

Be there. If you spend most of your days couped up in a closed office, you've got your priorities the wrong way round. Hang out with your people a little more.

#2
UNAPPRECIATED AND UNRECOGNISED

Here's what I've noticed. When I'm on a bus, each passenger thanks the driver as they alight at their stop – even though they've already paid their fare. During wedding speeches, the groom always comments on how beautiful the bridesmaids look – even when they don't.

So it's not that we're *incapable* of thanking and recognising people. We do it all the time. It's just that employees rank lower than bus drivers and unglamorous bridesmaids.

It doesn't matter how butch or macho or manly you are. This is not a fluffy, girly thing to do. This is a fundamental human need, no matter what your culture, gender, or age.

Sure, there are some managers who have a level of emotional intelligence on par with a doorknob, so the following guide may come as something new, but it certainly won't come as a struggle. Providing praise and recognition is actually quite easy. See for yourself:

Do it *quickly* – as soon as the good deed is done. Do it *face-to-face* – not through someone else or via email. Be *genuine* – mean what you say. Be *proactive* – be on the lookout for employees doing things right. Be *detailed* – rather than offering a vague 'well done'. And do it *positively* – don't mix it in with negative feedback.

If a single day goes by that you have not thanked or recognised at least one of your employees, you've failed in your job as a manager. It's that simple.

#1 LAZY AND UNDERPERFORMING CO-WORKERS

'**Never keep up with the Joneses. Drag them down to your level; it's cheaper.**' Quentin Crisp said that back in 1999. And it's a philosophy that underperforming employees are following at work. Rather than being inspired to perform as well as their successful peers, they instead choose to wallow in a pit of mediocrity.

Perhaps talented employees are so bothered by this because they see their incompetent colleagues getting paid close to or as much as they are – even though they're performing twice as well. In most companies, people get paid just for turning up rather than solely on how they perform.

The biggest mistake managers make is to spend too much time with underperforming employees, all the while thinking that their talented employees are okay. It's the *best* employees you should be dedicating your time to the most. For the rest:

Train them. Offer one-on-one coaching, courses, or on-the-job development. Give them a book, a CD, a DVD, or an online program. They need to be *switched on*.

Motivate them. Perhaps they need to be *intrinsically* motivated. Find out what fires them up inside and bring this alive at work. They need to be *turned on*.

Nurture them. Maybe the environment is the problem. Make sure they've got the resources, tools, and systems to be able to do their work. They need to be *kept on*.

Sack them. Failing the above, it's time to say so long and farewell. They need to be *moved on*.

UNCENSORED

Minute by minute, hour after hour, day by day, I endlessly analysed responses from thousands of employees. What made this slow and arduous exercise quite enjoyable was reading some of the brutally honest comments I encountered. I thought I'd share with you the ones that made me laugh out loud, the ones that made me think 'they can't be serious', and of course the just plain nutty ones.

The question they were asked was: *'What makes you angry, upset, or frustrated at work?'*

- 'The troll that sits three desks up from me that thinks she knows everything.'
- 'I believe that work is overrated and unnecessary. Humans work too hard for too little. The system is wrong.'

- 'My colleague has a voice like fingernails on a chalkboard. She speaks to me and everyone as if we're children and not quite bright. She reminds us regularly that she has a master's degree or a degree in this or that to make her point. She stares at me from odd places in the room, and watches what I'm doing. She magnifies her every ailment, coughing very loud with her mouth wide open, or sneezes with a huge "ACHOOOO," and if you say "bless you," she's off and running again about all her ailments. She's negative about everything. She always eats in my office and she smacks and slurps and stares at me.'

More uncensored...

- 'When I greet my manager with, "Good morning!" he replies with, "Is it?" He brings the morale of the whole mill down. He also yells at his subordinates and throws things. He is poison!'
- 'My business partner makes me angry because she is hopeless at just about everything to do with running the business. She admits that she is useless and is grateful to have me to do everything.'
- 'Always being told what to do, being bossed around, shouted at, talked about behind my back, being ostracised, not being trained, when other people withhold information, rudeness of clients, being rushed, being called in at short notice, having to work weekends, when co-workers or my boss are

not talkative, rude or unfriendly, when I am paid low, when my skills, abilities and achievements are not acknowledged, when I am not given enough hours. All this makes it a nightmare to work!'
- 'The managers who gossip as if their life depended on it ... Oftentimes their subordinates confide in them with personal matters. You would think that they would have the decency to keep their discussion confidential. Oh no! That is asking too much. It becomes a company headline.'
- 'My manager had little compassion for anyone and would often tell us that if we didn't agree with her every move, we did not belong on her team.'

And more ...
- 'What makes me really angry is when I answer a phone call asking me for a contact number they might need. Sure, I then read out the number and they ask me to hang on a second while they go and get a pen and paper.'
- 'Daily, my hope is to never be angry except with someone who is blaspheming God. With God's help, I walk in obedience to his commands, which include 1 Thessalonians 5:16-18 – rejoice evermore. Pray without ceasing. In everything give thanks for this is the will of God in Christ Jesus concerning you.'
- 'I find that my co-workers are the counsellors from Hell. They berate the clients, cussing at them, yelling,

humiliating them in front of others, and generally making these clients feel bad. The management is aware of this behaviour but refuses to do anything.'
- 'I dislike people who do not know how to be hygienic in the toilets.'
- 'I am not a piece of furniture, and if I'm giving you "time for dollars", calling my name once in a while goes a long way.'
- 'It's very hard to soar like an eagle when surrounded by turkeys.'
- 'When managers brag to each other in front of subordinates about the money they make.'
- 'I get upset when I say "Good morning" to my co-workers and they ignore me or act like they didn't hear me.'
- 'I get angry at work if people blame their dog for their own mistakes.'
- 'I am going to burn the place to the ground.'